Fresh from the Garden: 50 Vegetable Recipes

By: Kelly Johnson

Table of Contents

- Grilled Vegetable Skewers
- Ratatouille
- Stuffed Bell Peppers
- Creamy Broccoli Soup
- Zucchini Noodles with Pesto
- Roasted Brussels Sprouts with Balsamic Glaze
- Eggplant Parmesan
- Spinach and Mushroom Quiche
- Sweet Potato Fries
- Classic Gazpacho
- Roasted Cauliflower Steaks
- Spaghetti Squash with Marinara
- Grilled Asparagus with Lemon Butter
- Beet and Goat Cheese Salad
- Kale Chips
- Stuffed Portobello Mushrooms
- Creamed Spinach
- Butternut Squash Risotto
- Cabbage Stir-Fry
- Roasted Carrot and Ginger Soup
- Green Bean Almondine
- Baked Zucchini Fries
- Cauliflower Fried Rice
- Grilled Corn on the Cob
- Sweet Potato and Black Bean Tacos
- Pickled Vegetables
- Broccoli Salad with Cranberries
- Vegetable Stir-Fry with Soy Sauce
- Lentil and Veggie Shepherd's Pie
- Roasted Root Vegetables
- Spinach and Artichoke Dip
- Cucumber and Tomato Salad
- Roasted Garlic Mashed Cauliflower
- Shaved Fennel Salad

- Braised Leeks
- Acorn Squash with Maple Glaze
- Sautéed Swiss Chard
- Caramelized Onion Tart
- Grilled Eggplant Rolls
- Classic Caprese Salad
- Ratatouille Stuffed Zucchini
- Arugula and Pear Salad
- Heirloom Tomato Bruschetta
- Rainbow Veggie Buddha Bowl
- Garlic Roasted Mushrooms
- Avocado and Veggie Sushi Rolls
- Vegetarian Stuffed Cabbage Rolls
- Creamy Potato Leek Soup
- Vegan Spinach Lasagna
- Roasted Pumpkin with Spices

Grilled Vegetable Skewers

Ingredients:

- Assorted vegetables (bell peppers, zucchini, mushrooms, cherry tomatoes, onion)
- 3 tablespoons olive oil
- 1 teaspoon garlic powder
- 1 teaspoon dried oregano
- Salt and pepper, to taste
- Wooden or metal skewers

Instructions:

1. If using wooden skewers, soak them in water for 30 minutes to prevent burning.
2. Cut vegetables into evenly sized pieces for grilling.
3. In a bowl, toss vegetables with olive oil, garlic powder, oregano, salt, and pepper.
4. Thread the vegetables onto skewers.
5. Grill over medium heat for 10-12 minutes, turning occasionally until charred and tender.

Ratatouille

Ingredients:

- 1 eggplant, diced
- 2 zucchinis, diced
- 1 red bell pepper, diced
- 1 yellow bell pepper, diced
- 1 onion, chopped
- 4 tomatoes, diced
- 3 garlic cloves, minced
- 3 tablespoons olive oil
- 1 teaspoon dried thyme
- Salt and pepper, to taste

Instructions:

1. Heat olive oil in a large pan over medium heat.
2. Sauté onion and garlic until fragrant.
3. Add eggplant and cook for 5 minutes.
4. Stir in zucchini, bell peppers, tomatoes, thyme, salt, and pepper.
5. Cover and simmer for 20-25 minutes, stirring occasionally.

Stuffed Bell Peppers

Ingredients:

- 4 large bell peppers (any color)
- 1 cup cooked rice or quinoa
- 1 cup black beans or ground meat (optional)
- 1 cup diced tomatoes
- 1/2 cup shredded cheese
- 1 teaspoon paprika
- Salt and pepper, to taste

Instructions:

1. Preheat oven to 375°F (190°C).
2. Cut the tops off the bell peppers and remove seeds.
3. Mix rice, beans or meat, tomatoes, cheese, paprika, salt, and pepper in a bowl.
4. Stuff the mixture into the peppers and place them in a baking dish.
5. Cover with foil and bake for 25-30 minutes. Remove foil and bake an additional 5 minutes.

Creamy Broccoli Soup

Ingredients:

- 2 tablespoons butter
- 1 onion, chopped
- 3 cups broccoli florets
- 3 cups vegetable broth
- 1 cup heavy cream or milk
- Salt and pepper, to taste

Instructions:

1. Melt butter in a pot over medium heat and sauté onion until soft.
2. Add broccoli and vegetable broth. Bring to a boil, then simmer for 15 minutes.
3. Use an immersion blender to puree the soup until smooth.
4. Stir in cream, salt, and pepper. Heat gently before serving.

Zucchini Noodles with Pesto

Ingredients:

- 2 zucchinis, spiralized
- 1/4 cup pesto sauce
- 1 tablespoon olive oil
- 1/4 cup grated Parmesan cheese
- Salt and pepper, to taste

Instructions:

1. Heat olive oil in a skillet over medium heat.
2. Add zucchini noodles and sauté for 2-3 minutes.
3. Stir in pesto sauce and cook for 1 minute.
4. Sprinkle with Parmesan cheese, salt, and pepper before serving.

Roasted Brussels Sprouts with Balsamic Glaze

Ingredients:

- 1 lb Brussels sprouts, halved
- 2 tablespoons olive oil
- Salt and pepper, to taste
- 2 tablespoons balsamic glaze

Instructions:

1. Preheat oven to 400°F (200°C).
2. Toss Brussels sprouts with olive oil, salt, and pepper.
3. Spread on a baking sheet and roast for 20-25 minutes, stirring once.
4. Drizzle with balsamic glaze before serving.

Eggplant Parmesan

Ingredients:

- 1 large eggplant, sliced
- 1 cup breadcrumbs
- 1/2 cup grated Parmesan cheese
- 2 eggs, beaten
- 1 jar marinara sauce
- 1 cup shredded mozzarella cheese

Instructions:

1. Preheat oven to 375°F (190°C).
2. Dip eggplant slices into eggs, then coat with breadcrumbs mixed with Parmesan cheese.
3. Arrange slices on a baking sheet and bake for 15 minutes on each side.
4. Layer baked eggplant, marinara sauce, and mozzarella in a baking dish.
5. Bake for 20 minutes until bubbly.

Spinach and Mushroom Quiche

Ingredients:

- 1 pie crust
- 1 tablespoon butter
- 1 cup sliced mushrooms
- 2 cups fresh spinach
- 4 eggs
- 1 cup milk or cream
- 1/2 cup shredded cheese (Swiss or cheddar)
- Salt and pepper, to taste

Instructions:

1. Preheat oven to 375°F (190°C).
2. Heat butter in a skillet and sauté mushrooms and spinach until wilted.
3. Whisk eggs, milk, cheese, salt, and pepper in a bowl.
4. Spread spinach and mushrooms in the pie crust and pour the egg mixture on top.
5. Bake for 30-35 minutes or until set.

Sweet Potato Fries

Ingredients:

- 2 large sweet potatoes, peeled and cut into fries
- 2 tablespoons olive oil
- 1 teaspoon paprika
- 1/2 teaspoon garlic powder
- Salt and pepper, to taste

Instructions:

1. Preheat oven to 425°F (220°C).
2. Toss sweet potato fries with olive oil, paprika, garlic powder, salt, and pepper.
3. Spread fries on a baking sheet in a single layer.
4. Bake for 20-25 minutes, flipping halfway through, until crispy and golden brown.

Classic Gazpacho

Ingredients:

- 4 ripe tomatoes, chopped
- 1 cucumber, peeled and chopped
- 1 red bell pepper, chopped
- 1/4 red onion, chopped
- 2 garlic cloves, minced
- 3 tablespoons olive oil
- 2 tablespoons red wine vinegar
- Salt and pepper, to taste

Instructions:

1. Blend tomatoes, cucumber, bell pepper, onion, and garlic until smooth.
2. Add olive oil, red wine vinegar, salt, and pepper. Blend again.
3. Chill in the refrigerator for at least 2 hours before serving.

Roasted Cauliflower Steaks

Ingredients:

- 1 head cauliflower, sliced into 1-inch "steaks"
- 3 tablespoons olive oil
- 1 teaspoon smoked paprika
- Salt and pepper, to taste

Instructions:

1. Preheat oven to 400°F (200°C).
2. Brush cauliflower steaks with olive oil and season with paprika, salt, and pepper.
3. Place on a baking sheet and roast for 20-25 minutes, flipping halfway, until tender and golden.

Spaghetti Squash with Marinara

Ingredients:

- 1 spaghetti squash, halved and seeds removed
- 1 tablespoon olive oil
- 2 cups marinara sauce
- 1/4 cup grated Parmesan cheese
- Salt and pepper, to taste

Instructions:

1. Preheat oven to 400°F (200°C).
2. Rub the inside of the squash with olive oil, salt, and pepper. Place cut side down on a baking sheet.
3. Roast for 35-40 minutes, or until tender.
4. Scrape the flesh with a fork to create "spaghetti" strands. Top with marinara sauce and Parmesan.

Grilled Asparagus with Lemon Butter

Ingredients:

- 1 bunch asparagus, trimmed
- 2 tablespoons olive oil
- 2 tablespoons melted butter
- 1 teaspoon lemon juice
- Salt and pepper, to taste

Instructions:

1. Toss asparagus with olive oil, salt, and pepper.
2. Grill over medium heat for 5-7 minutes, turning occasionally.
3. Drizzle with melted butter and lemon juice before serving.

Beet and Goat Cheese Salad

Ingredients:

- 3 medium beets, roasted and sliced
- 4 cups mixed greens
- 1/4 cup crumbled goat cheese
- 1/4 cup candied walnuts
- 2 tablespoons balsamic glaze

Instructions:

1. Arrange greens on a plate and top with roasted beets, goat cheese, and walnuts.
2. Drizzle with balsamic glaze before serving.

Kale Chips

Ingredients:

- 1 bunch kale, stems removed and torn into pieces
- 2 tablespoons olive oil
- 1/2 teaspoon salt

Instructions:

1. Preheat oven to 300°F (150°C).
2. Toss kale with olive oil and salt.
3. Spread on a baking sheet in a single layer.
4. Bake for 20 minutes, or until crisp, checking to prevent burning.

Stuffed Portobello Mushrooms

Ingredients:

- 4 large Portobello mushrooms, stems removed
- 1 cup spinach, chopped
- 1/2 cup breadcrumbs
- 1/4 cup grated Parmesan cheese
- 1 clove garlic, minced
- 2 tablespoons olive oil
- Salt and pepper, to taste

Instructions:

1. Preheat oven to 375°F (190°C).
2. In a bowl, mix spinach, breadcrumbs, Parmesan, garlic, olive oil, salt, and pepper.
3. Spoon the mixture into the mushroom caps.
4. Place on a baking sheet and bake for 15-20 minutes, until tender and golden.

Creamed Spinach

Ingredients:

- 2 tablespoons butter
- 1 small onion, finely chopped
- 2 garlic cloves, minced
- 10 oz (300 g) fresh spinach, chopped
- 1/2 cup heavy cream
- 1/4 cup grated Parmesan cheese
- Salt and pepper, to taste

Instructions:

1. In a large skillet, melt butter over medium heat. Sauté onion and garlic until soft.
2. Add spinach and cook until wilted.
3. Stir in heavy cream and Parmesan cheese. Simmer for 2-3 minutes.
4. Season with salt and pepper before serving.

Butternut Squash Risotto

Ingredients:

- 1 cup Arborio rice
- 2 cups butternut squash, diced
- 4 cups vegetable broth, warmed
- 1 small onion, chopped
- 2 tablespoons olive oil
- 1/4 cup grated Parmesan cheese
- Salt and pepper, to taste

Instructions:

1. In a large pan, heat olive oil and sauté onion until translucent. Add rice and stir for 1-2 minutes.
2. Gradually add warm broth, 1/2 cup at a time, stirring until absorbed before adding more.
3. In a separate pan, sauté butternut squash until soft, then mash lightly.
4. Stir squash into the risotto and cook until creamy. Add Parmesan, salt, and pepper before serving.

Cabbage Stir-Fry

Ingredients:

- 4 cups green cabbage, shredded
- 1 tablespoon sesame oil
- 1 tablespoon soy sauce
- 2 garlic cloves, minced
- 1/2 teaspoon ginger, minced
- 1/2 teaspoon chili flakes (optional)

Instructions:

1. Heat sesame oil in a large skillet or wok over medium-high heat.
2. Add garlic, ginger, and chili flakes (if using) and sauté for 1 minute.
3. Add cabbage and stir-fry for 5-7 minutes until tender-crisp.
4. Drizzle with soy sauce, stir, and serve.

Roasted Carrot and Ginger Soup

Ingredients:

- 1 lb (450 g) carrots, peeled and chopped
- 1 small onion, chopped
- 1 tablespoon olive oil
- 1 teaspoon grated ginger
- 3 cups vegetable broth
- 1/2 cup coconut milk
- Salt and pepper, to taste

Instructions:

1. Preheat oven to 400°F (200°C). Toss carrots and onion with olive oil and roast for 25 minutes.
2. In a pot, combine roasted vegetables, ginger, and broth. Simmer for 10 minutes.
3. Blend until smooth, then stir in coconut milk.
4. Season with salt and pepper before serving.

Green Bean Almondine

Ingredients:

- 1 lb (450 g) green beans, trimmed
- 2 tablespoons butter
- 1/4 cup sliced almonds
- 1 garlic clove, minced
- Juice of 1/2 lemon
- Salt and pepper, to taste

Instructions:

1. Blanch green beans in boiling water for 3 minutes, then drain.
2. In a skillet, melt butter and toast almonds until golden.
3. Add garlic and green beans, sauté for 2-3 minutes.
4. Squeeze lemon juice over and season with salt and pepper before serving.

Baked Zucchini Fries

Ingredients:

- 2 zucchinis, cut into sticks
- 1/2 cup breadcrumbs
- 1/4 cup grated Parmesan cheese
- 1 egg, beaten
- 1 teaspoon Italian seasoning
- Salt and pepper, to taste

Instructions:

1. Preheat oven to 425°F (220°C). Line a baking sheet with parchment paper.
2. Mix breadcrumbs, Parmesan, Italian seasoning, salt, and pepper.
3. Dip zucchini sticks in egg, then coat in breadcrumb mixture.
4. Place on the baking sheet and bake for 20 minutes, flipping halfway.

Cauliflower Fried Rice

Ingredients:

- 1 medium head cauliflower, riced
- 2 tablespoons sesame oil
- 1 cup mixed vegetables (carrots, peas, etc.)
- 2 eggs, beaten
- 2 tablespoons soy sauce
- 1 green onion, chopped

Instructions:

1. Heat sesame oil in a large skillet. Sauté mixed vegetables until tender.
2. Push vegetables to one side, pour eggs into the skillet, and scramble.
3. Add cauliflower rice and soy sauce. Stir-fry for 5 minutes.
4. Garnish with green onion before serving.

Grilled Corn on the Cob

Ingredients:

- 4 ears of corn, husked
- 2 tablespoons butter, melted
- 1 teaspoon chili powder (optional)
- Salt and pepper, to taste

Instructions:

1. Preheat grill to medium-high heat.
2. Brush corn with melted butter and season with salt, pepper, and chili powder (if using).
3. Grill corn for 10-12 minutes, turning occasionally, until charred and tender.

Sweet Potato and Black Bean Tacos

Ingredients:

- 2 medium sweet potatoes, peeled and cubed
- 1 can (15 oz) black beans, drained and rinsed
- 2 tablespoons olive oil
- 1 teaspoon cumin
- 1 teaspoon chili powder
- 8 small corn or flour tortillas
- Toppings: avocado, salsa, cilantro

Instructions:

1. Preheat oven to 400°F (200°C). Toss sweet potato cubes with olive oil, cumin, and chili powder. Roast for 25-30 minutes.
2. Warm tortillas and fill with roasted sweet potatoes and black beans.
3. Add toppings of your choice and serve.

Pickled Vegetables

Ingredients:

- 2 cups mixed vegetables (carrots, radishes, cucumbers)
- 1 cup white vinegar
- 1/2 cup water
- 1 tablespoon sugar
- 1 teaspoon salt
- 1 teaspoon mustard seeds (optional)

Instructions:

1. Slice vegetables thinly and place in a clean jar.
2. In a saucepan, heat vinegar, water, sugar, salt, and mustard seeds until dissolved.
3. Pour over vegetables in the jar. Seal and refrigerate for at least 2 hours before serving.

Broccoli Salad with Cranberries

Ingredients:

- 2 cups broccoli florets, chopped
- 1/4 cup dried cranberries
- 1/4 cup sunflower seeds
- 1/4 cup red onion, finely diced
- 1/3 cup Greek yogurt
- 1 tablespoon honey
- 1 tablespoon apple cider vinegar

Instructions:

1. In a bowl, whisk together yogurt, honey, and vinegar for the dressing.
2. Combine broccoli, cranberries, sunflower seeds, and onion in a large bowl.
3. Toss with dressing and refrigerate for 15 minutes before serving.

Vegetable Stir-Fry with Soy Sauce

Ingredients:

- 1 tablespoon sesame oil
- 1 bell pepper, sliced
- 1 cup broccoli florets
- 1 cup snap peas
- 1 carrot, julienned
- 3 tablespoons soy sauce
- 1 teaspoon grated ginger

Instructions:

1. Heat sesame oil in a skillet or wok. Add all vegetables and stir-fry for 5-7 minutes.
2. Stir in soy sauce and ginger. Cook for an additional 2 minutes.
3. Serve over rice or noodles.

Lentil and Veggie Shepherd's Pie

Ingredients:

- 1 cup lentils, cooked
- 1 cup mixed vegetables (peas, carrots, corn)
- 2 cups mashed potatoes
- 1 tablespoon olive oil
- 1 small onion, diced
- 1 cup vegetable broth

Instructions:

1. Preheat oven to 375°F (190°C). Sauté onion in olive oil until soft.
2. Mix lentils, vegetables, and broth. Simmer for 5 minutes.
3. Transfer mixture to a baking dish and spread mashed potatoes on top.
4. Bake for 20 minutes, or until golden brown on top.

Roasted Root Vegetables

Ingredients:

- 2 carrots, peeled and chopped
- 2 parsnips, peeled and chopped
- 1 sweet potato, cubed
- 1 red onion, quartered
- 2 tablespoons olive oil
- 1 teaspoon rosemary
- Salt and pepper, to taste

Instructions:

1. Preheat oven to 400°F (200°C). Toss vegetables with olive oil, rosemary, salt, and pepper.
2. Spread on a baking sheet and roast for 30-35 minutes, stirring halfway through.

Spinach and Artichoke Dip

Ingredients:

- 1 cup fresh spinach, chopped
- 1 cup canned artichoke hearts, chopped
- 1/2 cup cream cheese
- 1/4 cup grated Parmesan cheese
- 1/4 cup sour cream
- 1 garlic clove, minced

Instructions:

1. Preheat oven to 375°F (190°C). Mix all ingredients in a bowl.
2. Transfer to an oven-safe dish and bake for 15-20 minutes, until bubbly.
3. Serve with crackers or bread.

Cucumber and Tomato Salad

Ingredients:

- 2 cups cucumber, sliced
- 1 cup cherry tomatoes, halved
- 2 tablespoons olive oil
- 1 tablespoon red wine vinegar
- 1 teaspoon dried oregano
- Salt and pepper, to taste

Instructions:

1. Combine cucumber and tomatoes in a bowl.
2. Whisk together olive oil, vinegar, oregano, salt, and pepper. Pour over the salad and toss well.

Roasted Garlic Mashed Cauliflower

Ingredients:

- 1 head of cauliflower, cut into florets
- 6 cloves garlic, peeled
- 1 tbsp olive oil
- 1/4 cup milk or cream
- 2 tbsp butter
- Salt and pepper to taste

Instructions:

1. Preheat the oven to 400°F (200°C).
2. Place the cauliflower florets and garlic on a baking sheet, drizzle with olive oil, and season with salt and pepper.
3. Roast for 20-25 minutes, until the cauliflower is tender and golden.
4. Transfer to a food processor, add milk or cream and butter, and blend until smooth.
5. Adjust seasoning with salt and pepper, then serve.

Shaved Fennel Salad

Ingredients:

- 1 fennel bulb, thinly sliced
- 1/4 cup fresh lemon juice
- 2 tbsp olive oil
- 1 tbsp honey
- Salt and pepper to taste
- Fresh parsley, chopped (for garnish)

Instructions:

1. Thinly shave the fennel bulb using a mandolin or sharp knife.
2. In a small bowl, whisk together lemon juice, olive oil, honey, salt, and pepper.
3. Toss the fennel with the dressing and let it sit for about 10 minutes to absorb the flavors.
4. Garnish with chopped parsley before serving.

Braised Leeks

Ingredients:

- 4 leeks, trimmed and halved
- 2 tbsp olive oil
- 1 cup vegetable or chicken broth
- 1/2 tsp thyme leaves
- Salt and pepper to taste

Instructions:

1. Heat olive oil in a large skillet over medium heat.
2. Add the leeks, cut side down, and cook until golden brown, about 5 minutes.
3. Flip the leeks and add the broth and thyme.
4. Cover and simmer for 20-25 minutes, until the leeks are tender.
5. Season with salt and pepper, then serve.

Acorn Squash with Maple Glaze

Ingredients:

- 2 acorn squash, halved and seeded
- 3 tbsp maple syrup
- 2 tbsp olive oil
- 1/2 tsp cinnamon
- Salt and pepper to taste

Instructions:

1. Preheat the oven to 375°F (190°C).
2. Place the squash halves on a baking sheet, cut side up.
3. In a small bowl, whisk together maple syrup, olive oil, cinnamon, salt, and pepper.
4. Drizzle the mixture over the squash.
5. Roast for 30-35 minutes, until the squash is tender and caramelized.

Sautéed Swiss Chard

Ingredients:

- 1 bunch Swiss chard, chopped
- 2 tbsp olive oil
- 2 cloves garlic, minced
- 1/4 tsp red pepper flakes (optional)
- Salt and pepper to taste

Instructions:

1. Heat olive oil in a large skillet over medium heat.
2. Add garlic and sauté for 1-2 minutes, until fragrant.
3. Add the Swiss chard and red pepper flakes (if using), and sauté for 5-7 minutes, until wilted.
4. Season with salt and pepper, and serve.

Caramelized Onion Tart

Ingredients:

- 1 sheet puff pastry
- 2 large onions, thinly sliced
- 2 tbsp olive oil
- 1/4 cup heavy cream
- 1/4 cup grated Gruyère cheese
- Salt and pepper to taste

Instructions:

1. Preheat the oven to 400°F (200°C).
2. Heat olive oil in a pan over low heat and add onions.
3. Cook the onions for 25-30 minutes, stirring occasionally, until caramelized.
4. Roll out the puff pastry on a baking sheet and prick with a fork.
5. Spread the caramelized onions over the pastry, drizzle with cream, and top with Gruyère cheese.
6. Bake for 20-25 minutes, until golden and crispy.

Grilled Eggplant Rolls

Ingredients:

- 2 eggplants, sliced lengthwise into 1/4-inch thick strips
- 1/2 cup ricotta cheese
- 1/4 cup basil pesto
- Olive oil for grilling
- Salt and pepper to taste

Instructions:

1. Preheat the grill to medium heat.
2. Brush the eggplant slices with olive oil and season with salt and pepper.
3. Grill the eggplant for 3-4 minutes per side, until tender and grill marks appear.
4. Spread a small amount of ricotta cheese and pesto on each eggplant slice.
5. Roll them up and secure with toothpicks.
6. Serve warm.

Classic Caprese Salad

Ingredients:

- 4 ripe tomatoes, sliced
- 1 ball fresh mozzarella, sliced
- 1/4 cup fresh basil leaves
- 2 tbsp olive oil
- 1 tbsp balsamic vinegar
- Salt and pepper to taste

Instructions:

1. Arrange the tomato and mozzarella slices on a platter.
2. Tuck basil leaves between the slices.
3. Drizzle with olive oil and balsamic vinegar.
4. Season with salt and pepper, then serve.

Ratatouille Stuffed Zucchini

Ingredients:

- 4 zucchinis, halved and hollowed out
- 1 small eggplant, diced
- 1 bell pepper, diced
- 1 tomato, diced
- 1/4 cup olive oil
- 1/2 tsp thyme
- Salt and pepper to taste

Instructions:

1. Preheat the oven to 375°F (190°C).
2. In a skillet, heat olive oil and sauté the eggplant, bell pepper, and tomato for 5-7 minutes, until tender.
3. Stir in thyme, salt, and pepper.
4. Stuff the zucchini halves with the ratatouille mixture and place them on a baking sheet.
5. Bake for 20-25 minutes, until the zucchini is tender.

Arugula and Pear Salad

Ingredients:

- 4 cups fresh arugula
- 2 pears, sliced
- 1/4 cup crumbled blue cheese
- 1/4 cup candied pecans
- 1 tbsp olive oil
- 1 tbsp balsamic vinegar
- Salt and pepper to taste

Instructions:

1. In a large bowl, combine the arugula, pear slices, blue cheese, and candied pecans.
2. In a small bowl, whisk together olive oil, balsamic vinegar, salt, and pepper.
3. Drizzle the dressing over the salad and toss gently.
4. Serve immediately.

Heirloom Tomato Bruschetta

Ingredients:

- 4 heirloom tomatoes, diced
- 1/4 cup fresh basil, chopped
- 2 cloves garlic, minced
- 1 tbsp balsamic vinegar
- 1 tbsp olive oil
- Salt and pepper to taste
- 1 baguette, sliced and toasted

Instructions:

1. In a bowl, combine the tomatoes, basil, garlic, balsamic vinegar, olive oil, salt, and pepper.
2. Let the mixture sit for 10 minutes to meld the flavors.
3. Spoon the tomato mixture onto the toasted baguette slices.
4. Serve immediately.

Rainbow Veggie Buddha Bowl

Ingredients:

- 1 cup cooked quinoa
- 1/2 cup roasted sweet potatoes, cubed
- 1/2 cup roasted chickpeas
- 1/2 cup steamed broccoli
- 1/4 cup shredded carrots
- 1/4 avocado, sliced
- 2 tbsp tahini
- 1 tbsp lemon juice
- Salt and pepper to taste

Instructions:

1. In a bowl, arrange the cooked quinoa as the base.
2. Layer the roasted sweet potatoes, chickpeas, steamed broccoli, shredded carrots, and avocado on top.
3. In a small bowl, whisk together tahini, lemon juice, salt, and pepper.
4. Drizzle the tahini sauce over the bowl and serve.

Garlic Roasted Mushrooms

Ingredients:

- 2 cups button mushrooms, cleaned and halved
- 3 cloves garlic, minced
- 2 tbsp olive oil
- 1 tsp thyme
- Salt and pepper to taste

Instructions:

1. Preheat the oven to 400°F (200°C).
2. In a bowl, toss the mushrooms with olive oil, garlic, thyme, salt, and pepper.
3. Spread the mushrooms on a baking sheet in a single layer.
4. Roast for 15-20 minutes, until tender and golden.
5. Serve immediately.

Avocado and Veggie Sushi Rolls

Ingredients:

- 1 cup sushi rice, cooked
- 4 sheets nori (seaweed)
- 1/2 avocado, sliced
- 1/2 cucumber, julienned
- 1/4 red bell pepper, julienned
- Soy sauce for dipping

Instructions:

1. Place a nori sheet on a bamboo sushi mat, shiny side down.
2. Spread a thin layer of sushi rice over the nori, leaving a small border at the top.
3. Arrange avocado, cucumber, and bell pepper along the bottom edge of the rice.
4. Roll the sushi tightly from the bottom, using the mat to help.
5. Slice the roll into 6-8 pieces and serve with soy sauce.

Vegetarian Stuffed Cabbage Rolls

Ingredients:

- 12 cabbage leaves, blanched
- 1 cup cooked rice
- 1 cup cooked lentils
- 1/2 cup diced onions
- 2 cloves garlic, minced
- 1 can crushed tomatoes
- 1 tsp dried oregano
- 1 tbsp olive oil
- Salt and pepper to taste

Instructions:

1. Preheat the oven to 350°F (175°C).
2. In a pan, heat olive oil and sauté the onions and garlic until soft.
3. Add cooked rice, lentils, oregano, salt, and pepper, and stir to combine.
4. Place a spoonful of the filling onto each cabbage leaf and roll tightly.
5. Place the rolls in a baking dish, pour crushed tomatoes over them, and cover with foil.
6. Bake for 30-35 minutes.
7. Serve warm.

Creamy Potato Leek Soup

Ingredients:

- 3 large potatoes, peeled and diced
- 2 leeks, cleaned and sliced
- 4 cups vegetable broth
- 1 cup heavy cream
- 2 tbsp butter
- Salt and pepper to taste
- Fresh chives for garnish

Instructions:

1. In a large pot, melt butter over medium heat and sauté the leeks until soft, about 5 minutes.
2. Add the diced potatoes and vegetable broth. Bring to a boil, then reduce to a simmer.
3. Cook for 15-20 minutes, until the potatoes are tender.
4. Use an immersion blender to puree the soup until smooth.
5. Stir in the heavy cream and season with salt and pepper.
6. Serve garnished with fresh chives.

Vegan Spinach Lasagna

Ingredients:

- 9 lasagna noodles, cooked
- 4 cups fresh spinach, chopped
- 1 cup ricotta-style vegan cheese
- 1 1/2 cups marinara sauce
- 1/4 cup nutritional yeast
- 1 tbsp olive oil
- 1/2 tsp dried oregano
- Salt and pepper to taste

Instructions:

1. Preheat the oven to 375°F (190°C).
2. In a pan, heat olive oil and sauté the spinach until wilted.
3. In a bowl, combine the sautéed spinach, vegan ricotta cheese, nutritional yeast, oregano, salt, and pepper.
4. In a baking dish, spread a thin layer of marinara sauce. Layer the cooked lasagna noodles, spinach mixture, and sauce. Repeat for 3 layers.
5. Top with marinara sauce and bake for 25-30 minutes.
6. Let it cool slightly before serving.

Roasted Pumpkin with Spices

Ingredients:

- 1 small pumpkin, peeled and cubed
- 2 tbsp olive oil
- 1 tsp ground cinnamon
- 1/2 tsp ground nutmeg
- Salt and pepper to taste

Instructions:

1. Preheat the oven to 375°F (190°C).
2. Toss the pumpkin cubes with olive oil, cinnamon, nutmeg, salt, and pepper.
3. Spread the pumpkin in a single layer on a baking sheet.
4. Roast for 25-30 minutes, stirring halfway through, until tender and caramelized.
5. Serve warm.